Little Shop of Flowers

～ ❀ ～

A.k.a. the Thrift Shop

Marjorie Burke

authorHOUSE®

AuthorHouse™
1663 Liberty Drive
Bloomington, IN 47403
www.authorhouse.com
Phone: 1 (800) 839-8640

Published by AuthorHouse 07/26/2018

ISBN: 978-1-5462-5205-4 (sc)
ISBN: 978-1-5462-5204-7 (e)

Library of Congress Control Number: 2018908497

Print information available on the last page.

Contents

Dedication

This book is dedicated to volunteers at thrift shops everywhere. These people not only perform a service to their community, but also fill a need in themselves by doing something productive with their free time. While they work to raise money for a good cause, they also often lend an ear to people who seem to need someone to talk to. Some are just normal folks, others not so normal.

Preface

The idea for this book all started several years ago when my granddaughters were young and I was called upon occasionally to "babysit." When they were old enough to entertain themselves for awhile, I sat down at my son's computer and started jotting down stories about the Thrift Shop, where I had been volunteering since retirement.

While the idea for the book stayed on a "back burner" it was always there simmering. The longer I volunteered at the shop, the more stories I wrote. One day after emailing and texting my son with various questions about how to get a photo from my iPad onto Facebook or what to do when my solitaire game page came up blank, he said, "Mother, you need to find something to do." So, I got serious about the book, and herein lies the result.

I have given the "bouquet" of dedicated lady volunteers made-up flowery names to match their personalities or character. You'll meet Rosie Sharoni, the spunky Italian, Dora Bell, the chairwoman who has a funny sense of style, Scarlet Sage, the redhead with her words of wisdom, Hosta LaSeeya, the clothes person, who gets her leaves in a flutter, and our storyteller,

Mari Gold, who makes a big deal over everything, especially decorating the windows. Hazel Whisp, Shammy O'Rock, Susie Black, Sweet Alyssa and Lu Pine also make appearances.

Characters who visit the shop on a regular basis include the paranoid Jack Backpack, the charmer Big Mike, a joke-telling priest named Spiro, the entertaining Eddie the Trivia Guy, and Tricky Dick, who scams 90-year old Violet.

There's Chatty Cathy, who just hangs out, the Poor Soul, who carries on conversations with no one in particular, Waltzing Matilda, who likes to try on and model clothes, and the Shuffler.

The book is strictly written in fun and is not intended to hurt anyone in any way. It's a bunch of stories about older ladies who are retired, widowed, or who just want to do something useful with their free time. The stories are also about the people they encounter at the Thrift Shop. They often find themselves sharing life experiences with customers who are looking for bargains, or just listening to lonely people who need a place to go or someone to talk to.

And here, I would like to thank my dear daughter for listening to all my stories, proofreading the book, and running off the hard copies.

Mari Gold's Introduction

One lovely fall day, having recently retired, a lady who will be known herein as Mari Gold was taking a leisurely stroll down the Main Street of Milltown, the little place she calls home. As she passed the small places of business, she took note of the people inside, and those coming and going. Having resided and worked in the town for 30 years, she regularly saw people she knew when she was out and about.

Mari Gold saw a familiar face behind the counter inside the local Thrift Shop. The face was that of a former customer of hers from the paint and wallpaper store from where she had retired after 20 years. So she decided to stop in to say hello.

A tall, bald-headed man stood at the counter, talking loudly in a thick foreign accent. He seemed to be causing a bit of commotion. A mountain of merchandise, topped off with a wedding dress, was heaped up in front of the counter.

"Hi Rosie, how are things going?" Mari Gold asked. Rosie rolled her heavily massacred and blue shadowed eyes and heaved a big sigh. Mari Gold commented that it seemed Rosie had her hands full, to which Rosie commented, "You can say that again."

She referred to the man before her as a "crazy so and so," and said something to the effect that he was buying up "everything in the place." Rosie definitely appeared to be exasperated.

Mari Gold asked the man what he planned to do with all the things he was buying. Seeming somewhat annoyed by her question, the man waved his arms around wildly, and stated that he planned to give it all away to neighbors, friends and whoever else he chose.

Mari Gold asked Rosie if she would like some help. Rosie said it would be great to have a helping hand with bagging the items while she tallied up the sales. She needed to enter everything in the sales book "and figure out what this son-of-a-b owes."

Mari Gold began helping her friend, but bagging the man's purchases was turning into quite a chore. There really weren't any bags or containers large enough to hold everything. She asked the customer where he was parked, to which he replied, "just across the street." She asked if it would be all right if she helped carry the larger items out to the car. He said, "Yeah, sure."

As Rosie itemized the various dishes, pots and pans, knick knacks, glassware, books and clothes, and the wedding dress, Mari Gold helped "the Hungarian" as he came to be known, take the things out to his car. She noticed immediately that his car was packed full and didn't think there was enough room for everything. He told her to just "stuff it in," insisting that it would all fit. Mari Gold cautioned that it was illegal to drive a car when the visibility was impaired, and that he was risking being stopped by the police. The Hungarian brushed off the comment, stating that he wasn't worried. After somehow managing to get everything into the vehicle, the man returned to the shop, Mari Gold in tow, and asked Rosie how much he owed.

"Two hundred three dollars. Now get it up, and fast," Rosie demanded, as only she could get away with. "I'm trying to get out of here! We close at 4, you know." The bald-headed man laughed, saying he loved bold women. He asked if he could take her out to dinner sometime.

"Thanks, but no thanks," Rosie said in a pleasant but definite refusal, adding that she was a widow, but wasn't desperate. She then proceeded to put the money from the day's sales in an envelope and escorted the man to the front door. As she locked the door behind him, she turned to Mari Gold and said, "Now let's get the hell out of here!"

Mari Gold asked if the man came to the shop often, to which Rosie replied that he had just recently become a customer. "Don't know where in the bejesus he came from," Rosie said, adding that the man told her he was from Hungary. She added that the other ladies who worked in the shop didn't like dealing with him, that he made them nervous. "He doesn't scare me, Rosie said with a chuckle. "You know me. I can handle anybody."

As Mari Gold walked with Rosie to her car, she asked how long she had worked at the shop. Rosie said she started volunteering there after her husband died, as she was looking for ways to stay occupied. She really missed her husband. Mari Gold discovered in time that several of the women who volunteered at the shop were widows. Most of the volunteers were retired and had free time on their hands. Some had been nurses and since the Thrift Shop was in operation for the benefit of the local hospital, volunteering there appealed to them.

Mari Gold asked Rosie if the shop needed help. Rosie told her they were always looking for help, pointing out that it was strictly volunteer work and there weren't too many people out there "dumb enough" to work for nothing. Mari Gold said she might like to try it and wondered who she needed to talk to. That's when Rosie said, "Leave it to me, kiddo. As far as I'm concerned you're in!" That was about ten years ago.

A couple of notes here:

Shortly after the day Mari Gold encountered the man from Hungary, she was browsing a consignment shop in town. She mentioned the rather strange fellow to the owner of the consignment shop since she knew her and had done business there. The woman said she thought it sounded like a rather odd fellow who had been in her store, usually wearing some disguise. One day, she believed it was he who came in wearing a wedding dress!

Also, a group of ladies who worked Tuesday mornings — the Four Leaf Clovers (two sisters, and friends of sisters) — related a story about their dealings with "the Hungarian." When the fourth clover first started volunteering, she hated to see this man come into the shop. "He'd make a mess," she said, "piling things he wanted to buy all over the counters. He was also very disruptive." One of the sisters said he was friendly toward her until she told him she was married to a man from Hungary. "After that" she said, "he didn't like me." She couldn't figure out why.

At some point, it was rumored that the man was barred from several businesses in town. It wasn't long afterwards that the ladies noticed he wasn't coming around any longer.

Some History

Thrift shops have probably been popular since their inception, some times more than others. They weren't always looked upon favorably by people of means who wouldn't think of being seen in or purchasing anything at such places. Today they seem to be as popular as ever. It doesn't hurt when a very knowledgeable, charming and quite entertaining contestant on a popular game show admits that he buys all his clothes at thrift shops.

Thrift stores date back to about 1820 and came into existence to help the needy, although today everyone from the poverty stricken to millionaires shop at them. Mari Gold contends that millionaires (not all, we're talking self-made here, not people born into wealth) exist because they are thrifty. They don't accumulate their millions by throwing money to the wind or spending their money foolishly.

Most people are familiar with Salvation Army and Goodwill Industries which have been around since 1879 and 1902 respectively. In the beginning, the Salvation Army was considered a junk dealer, thus a place people who could afford to buy at "real" stores would not shop. Goodwill Industries employed the poor and disabled who gathered goods for reuse. And then there were "Ragmen," around since the 1890's. They were generally looked upon unfavorably, but today are viewed as a valuable resource.

Thrift shops exist all over for the benefit of churches, schools, hospitals and such. The little Thrift Shop that is the scene of this story has been around for about 75 years, always on the Main Street, although it has occupied several locations. It amazes Mari Gold when a visitor says they've never been into the shop, or didn't know it was there.

Being thrifty used to be synonymous with being of little means or being "cheap." Mari Gold has often been accused by coworkers, and even her own children, of being cheap but she is quick to defend herself, saying that she has had to be careful with how she spends her money. She'd never pay big bucks for material things like designer clothes, expensive jewelry or luxury cars. To her it has nothing to do with being cheap but is just good common sense.

The definition of thrift found on Google is "the quality of using money and other resources carefully and not wastefully." According to Webster's New American Dictionary, copyright 1939, 1965, the number one definition for thrift is "Frugality, economical management."

Somewhere, sometime, someone—probably a wealthy woman— suggested that she and her friends could donate their "designer" clothes to be sold at a rummage sale to raise money for their church. Less well-off women discovered they could buy pricey clothes very reasonably. Eventually buying second-hand clothes was considered a good way to shop, and public opinion began to change with regard to shopping at places like thrift shops. It was helpful when, somewhere along the line, people who ran these shops started copying regular department stores using appealing displays for items of clothing, housewares and such.

Many visitors to the shop featured herein comment on what a nice little shop it is. That's been due to a few very dedicated volunteers who love working there and enjoy keeping things in order and displayed in a way that has been appealing. It wasn't always so neat and tidy. Years before Mari Gold became involved, she had visited the shop when donations were literally piled on tables. Clothes overflowed from plastic bags. Dishes and glassware were often in need of a wash. And the windows didn't look much better with items just thrown about willy nilly.

Some shoppers don't mind the junked-up look and rather enjoy plowing through heaps of discarded items. Mari Gold has been known to visit places like that, one being run by a fellow who is a "liquidator." His place once was a gas station and garage. It is now stuffed to the rafters with everything imaginable. Another place, which has since gone out of business, was run by a father and son. It was a borderline life-threatening experience to plow through the piles of "junk" they sold.

One of Mari Gold's favorite shows, which has been on television for several years, is about two fellows from Iowa who travel all over the country searching for old things. They climb up into the rafters of old barns and various buildings and sort through piles of a myriad of things that unusual people have collected for 20, 30, 40 years or more.

Today it seems hoards of people are into buying secondhand, even young people, who go for vintage clothing and midcentury modern. Yard sales have been around for years, but when people discovered they could consign their finds and make money, those type stores started opening up everywhere. Then came the internet which has several sites to list used articles for sale. Thrift shops are a great source for folks in this kind of business.

While this book was in its final stages, one of the popular morning shows did a segment on men's clothes. Hawaiian-print shirts apparently have become "all the rage." The ones featured on the program were pricey, at around $80 or $100. Mari Gold rounded up all the Hawaiian shirts she could find at the shop and hung them at the front of the shirt rack in the men's department. At the bargain price of $2.00, they were gone within a couple of days. Some, of course had been worn, but others were obviously new.

There will always be people who wouldn't think of using someone's else's cast-offs, but in Mari Gold's opinion, they just don't realize what they're missing.

The One and Only Rosie

So about 10 years ago, Mari Gold began working with Rosie on Tuesday afternoons. Rosie's lifelong friend, Petunia, had been working with her until her friend's husband became ill. The two women were rarely seen without the other. Petunia always allowed Rosie her entrance, following behind a step or two. She was as quiet as Rosie was vocal, and was definitely her "straight man."

When Mari Gold first began volunteering, Rosie told Mari Gold the story of how she met Petunia. When they were only about five or six years old, one day Rosie spotted "a little girl just sitting there on her front stoop, looking like she needed a friend." So Rosie crossed the street and asked her if she wanted to play. Rosie said back then the Italians and Irish didn't mingle, but she and Petunia became friends, and that was nearly 70 years ago. Rosie liked to say she was FBI, which to her meant "Full Blooded Italian" or "Full Breasted Italian." This claim was always accompanied with one of her raucous laughs.

Another time, when Rosie and Mari Gold were telling stories about their childhoods, Rosie shared that her father died when she was a young girl. Her mother moved the family from their home in New Jersey to Milltown where they had relatives. Rosie had a sister and two brothers and her mother figured it would be the only way she would be able to manage to take care of all of them. In the end, everything worked out fine.

Mari Gold told Rosie that her mother and father moved their family from Pennsylvania to California when she and her sister were only 6 and almost 8. So both women knew what it was like to make those kinds of adjustments as young girls.

She first met Rosie when she came to the wallpaper and paint store where Mari Gold worked before retiring. Rosie was shopping for wallpaper and had heard that Mari Gold was the person to see. Rosie spent quite a few hours in the store looking for just the right paper for her kitchen. She had in mind something with strawberries. Mari Gold helped her find just the right pattern. That wallpaper was still on the walls several years later when Mari Gold visited Rosie's home when she was recovering from surgery.

Rosie Sharoni was definitely a colorful character. She could have even been called flamboyant. Her namesake flower is a showy pink or purple, two of her favorite colors. She always wore a shade of bright pink or purple on her fingernails, although one year for Easter she painted them a bright yellow. All of her fingers donned rings with various stones. A hint of purple sometimes could be detected in her hair color. Mari Gold assumed that Rosie colored her hair at home since it seemed to vary in shades of black. She wore it short with little spirally curls for bangs.

Several gold chains with charms hung around her neck. She told Mari Gold they were all gifts from her husband or sister. She wore all of them everyday, saying that she was "very sen-ta-mental," placing emphasis on each syllable. Most of her mother's things remained in her second floor apartment, where her mother lived for several years before passing. Rosie admitted that she just couldn't seem to get rid of anything — a common habit of many of the volunteers and shoppers at the Thrift Shop.

Rosie liked to have music playing while she worked, although it was difficult to find a station that came in on the radio without a lot of static, probably because the shop was boxed in between other businesses and had lousy reception. When there were no customers, Rosie danced around the shop, snapping her fingers to the music. If the radio wasn't cooperating, she would sing. One of her favorite songs was "There were no angels til I met you." She said her husband used to sing it to her.

One afternoon Rosie began singing songs in alphabetical order. No lie, sang one song after another from A to Z with little hesitation. "Don't look at me with those bloodshot eyes" was certainly unusual!

Two ladies who Rosie called Thelma and Louise were frequent Tuesday afternoon visitors. Upon entering the shop Rosie would ask what they had been up to that day. Usually they had been shopping and out to lunch. Rosie would tell them how nice it was to see people dressed up. "We like to get dolled up once in awhile," Louise would say.

Then Rosie would be apt to ask if they'd "had any hot dates lately." Thelma reminded Rosie that she was married and Louise, who had lost her husband, wasn't having much luck. She said she wouldn't mind finding a nice man just to go out to dinner with once in awhile, but added with a wink that "They all want one thing, if you know what I mean. They always seem to expect a roll in the hay." Rosie's comeback: "You've got that right. And, you're lucky if they aren't in diapers."

Louise and Rosie reminisced about their deceased husbands, saying they were "the best," and how a good man only comes along once in a lifetime. Rosie, who married later than most of her friends, said she used to tell her mother she wanted a husband who could dance. Even though her mother told her she wouldn't be doing much dancing after she got married, Rosie held out. She was actually engaged to a man who did not dance when she met the man who ultimately became her husband. He loved to dance just as much as she did.

"The same thing happened to me!" Louise exclaimed. She always loved to dance, and was engaged to a man who didn't. At a party one time, a friend of Louise's fiancé noticed her tapping her feet and looking very much in the mood to dance. So he asked the fiancé if it would be all right if he danced with Louise. The fiancé said fine. Later, the fiancé moved away to a city where he and Louise were planning to live after they got married. During the separation, the fiancé's friend asked if it would be all right if he took Louise out dancing. A casual friendship turned serious, the engagement to the non-dancer was called off, and Louise eventually married the man who danced.

Rosie and Louise agreed that in both their cases, it had been a good thing they didn't marry the other guys. Somewhere over the years, they discovered the guys they had planned to marry turned out to be not-so-good husband material. When Rosie and Louise were finished reminiscing, Thelma would be ready to buy a blouse or scarf. "Where else can you find such a bargain?" Rosie would ask, and as they left the shop, Rosie always added, "Come back when you can spend more." The two women would bid farewell with a smile.

Closing time was 4 o'clock. If the shop wasn't busy, Rosie would lock up a few minutes early. At times, just as she was about to put the key in the door, a couple of her favorites, Rachel and Joe, would show up. She'd allow them to come in and look around as she enjoyed exchanging raunchy jokes with Rachel. On one occasion, Rosie asked if Rachel had been ill since it was evident she'd lost weight. Rachel explained that she had been on a diet. "I've been taking collagen to keep my skin from sagging," she said. She winked and said, "my husband just loves the new me," alluding to the fact that their sex life had improved.

It was usually worthwhile to stay open a few extra minutes as Rachel invariably spent $20 or $30, considered a good sale, given that most items only cost 50 cents or a $1.00. When they were ready to leave, Rosie would say, "next time don't wait til we're ready to close for crying out loud. Goodbye."

Sometimes she would add one of her standard lines, "I'll keep the faith. You keep the commandments."

Spiro

A Greek Priest, named Spiro, was another Tuesday afternoon regular, almost always with a joke to share. One day he asked if Mari Gold and Rosie had heard the one about "the guy who asked God for a chick with long legs?" The ladies admitted that they hadn't. So Spiro proceeded to tell them about the guy who was taking some libation at a local pub when an ostrich strolled up beside him and asked for a drink. When the barkeep asked, "what's with the ostrich?" the fellow rubbed his beard and said, "Geez, I guess this is what I get for asking the Good Lord to send me a chick with long legs. She isn't exactly what I had in mind."

Spiro browsed through the supply of greeting cards which were usually in good supply. He would comment that he still liked to send cards to people even though most people had given up the practice. "Me too," Mari Gold responded, stating that these days "everyone" seemed to resort to email instead. "It's the easy way out as far as I'm concerned," she'd say. Both agreed that it just was not the same as finding a real card in your mailbox.

"You certainly can't beat your prices," Spiro would say. The shop only charged ten cents per card, a real bargain given the going price at local card stores.

Since the custom of sending out birthday and anniversary cards just about had become as extinct as the dodo bird, bags and boxes of birthday and holiday cards were donated on a regular basis. Many came from collections of deceased family members.

When Spiro brought his "finds" to the counter, he'd take a look at the jewelry. It was displayed under the glass in the counter where the volunteers kept track of the sales and wrapped up the purchases. When he spotted something he liked, he would buy it, saying that he enjoyed giving something nice to the ladies at the nursing home where his wife was a resident.

On another visit, Spiro asked, "Have you ladies heard about the fellow who climbed onto his roof when the floodwaters came?" As usual, Mari Gold and Rosie said they had not. So Spiro continued.

"Well, there's this fellow up on his roof praying for God to rescue him. A man in a row boat comes by and tells the fellow to climb in. No, thank you, the fellow says. I'm waiting for the Good Lord to save me. All right then. Good luck. Next, a man in a speed boat roars up. Get in, he says. No thank you. I'm waiting for the Good Lord to save me. So the speed boat takes off. Awhile later, a helicopter hovering overhead, drops a rope. Grab on, the pilot says over a loud speaker. Again the man declines, stating that he's waiting for the Good Lord to save him. Eventually the floodwaters take the man down stream and he drowns. When he gets to heaven, he asks God why he didn't save him. God answers, I sent two boats and a helicopter. What were you expecting."

Spiro was certainly a delightful and welcome customer. When months passed without a visit from him, Rosie said she was pretty certain that he had passed away.

The Chairwoman

Historically the Thrift Shop had a chairman and a co-chairman, although it was more like a chairman and an assistant. One of the two usually took charge. Previous to the current "chairs," the woman who had been number one co-chair became ill and could no longer carry out her duties. Her co-chair didn't want the job, so replacements were needed in a hurry. Not an easy task. The then President of the Hospital Guild, which is responsible for the Thrift Shop, was thrown into a tizzy trying to find two new ladies who would actually agree to manage the shop. It came with a lot of responsibility, meant working with many volunteer women of advanced age, under one roof — the old saying about too many cooks in the kitchen comes to mind here. And, these were strictly volunteer positions.

Two women who had recently come on board agreed to step up. Their personalities were quite different, but they agreed they would work together.

Enter Dora Bell — this name chosen because it could be the name of a rare flower. Her hairstyle was similar to the one worn by the little Spanish explorer of children's books and cartoons, and she was so proud of her signs, printed in English and Spanish. After a short time in her new role, Dora announced that she did not need or want a co-chair, so the number two co-chair became the "assistant." This created a good bit of friction between the two.

Over her 70-plus years, Dora Bell had more than her fair share of life's challenges. She had asthma which at times caused her to be hospitalized. She had suffered with tremors for years and had brain surgery which involved having wires installed in her head — something like a pacemaker. This procedure reportedly helped to some extent but she continued to live with shaky hands, and was somewhat unsteady on her feet. The tremors made her handwriting extremely difficult to read. She joked about it though, referring to it as chicken scratch. Sometimes she'd say, "You mean you can't read my beautiful handwriting?" It was really quite illegible. She also joked about her position, saying, "You don't think I got this job based on my looks, do you?"

It was certainly helpful if the volunteers had a sense of humor — an area where Mari Gold would readily admit she fell short. A former co-worker of hers once told her about someone she considered funny, then commented, "but you, Mari, you aren't funny." "Gee, thanks," Mari Gold thought to herself. She always thought she could be funny, and she'd been told at times that she had a sense of humor.

Mari Gold wondered if it was Dora's sense of humor that drove her unique sense of fashion. A favorite item of clothing for quite awhile was a pair of denim capris embroidered with tiny red lobsters. She was overjoyed when she found them, as she claimed it was rare to find something she liked in her size.

One Halloween, Dora wore these capris with a white turtleneck printed with orange pumpkins. She apparently liked the combo enough to wear it off and on in the fall. When winter arrived, she still wore the capris, accompanied with heavy socks, boots and a parka with a fur-lined hood, which all apparently made up for the cropped pants exposing the bottom of her legs.

Dora readily admitted that she wasn't into fashion and had trouble distinguishing between a woman's blouse and a man's shirt.

One of Dora's favorite things was making signs. Using her computer, she printed out signs with pictures to correspond with items for sale, such as hats, gloves, shirts, books, etc. She was also proud of the fact that the signs attached to the various racks of clothes listed the articles with their prices in three languages: English, Spanish, and Portuguese. Many shop customers were from Puerto Rico, Columbia, Brazil and other Latin countries.

Printing the signs in these languages was all well and good, but the translations weren't always quite right. A Spanish-speaking woman, who visited the shop on a daily basis, often spouting off all sorts of advice about how things should be done in the shop, remarked that one of the signs wasn't worded correctly. In an effort to remove any doubt as to which language was being used, Dora adjusted the signs by using a different color print to identify each language.

Then there was Rosie, who attempted to speak in foreign tongues. She'd combine Italian with Spanish and some made up language to communicate with customers. She was convinced that they understood what she was saying because she'd ask them if they did and usually the customer would nod in the affirmative. It was pretty apparent to everyone else that they didn't have the slightest idea what she was saying, but just humored her. On one occasion a man went to his car to get some money. After several minutes Rosie said to his wife, "Where the bleep did he go? New York?" The customer obviously recognized the word "New York"" so she acted as if she understood. "See, she understands," Rosie boasted.

One of the shop's regulars was Big Mike (described later). One of his pals got Mari Gold one day. Mike said he didn't have any money. His friend looked at Mari Gold and asked, "you know how you say that in Italian? — mafundsalo." Mari Gold repeated it feeling proud she got the pronunciation, only to have the guy laugh. Then she got it.

Dora posted signs all over the shop. Signs instructing customers not to reach into the window for items, but to ask for assistance. Nonetheless, customers frequently leaned over the wooden pole, shirred with a curtain, to reach an item on display in the window. There were signs with instructions about what to do if a customer fell or got hurt. Dora was always just trying to be conscientious, but Mari Gold kept saying, "People don't read signs."

Mari Gold surely was a thorn in Dora Bell's side. And, she would have been the first to admit that she was bossy and strong willed. (Marigolds are known to be hardy, persistent and offensive to pests. Mari Gold was definitely not a delicate flower loved by everyone.) Dora never acted as though she was annoyed or irritated by her, however.

Still on the subject of signs, "Property of Thrift Shop" stickers were stuck to everything from the tape dispensers, staplers, carts, phones, hammers, jars of nails, etc. It had happened on more than one occasion that a volunteer who had stopped in for a visit, set down a jacket, umbrella, or pair of sun glasses on the counter, only to discover that a customer picked the item up, and bought it. Dora lost a favorite Red Sox scarf to a customer after leaving it on the counter unattended for just a couple of minutes. Mari Gold thought it was a little much though when "Property of Thrift Shop" stickers were plastered on counters which were so heavy it would have taken two or three teenage boys to budge them, let alone remove them from the shop.

Often women who expressed an interest in volunteering were unknown to Dora Bell — even when they were virtual pillars in the community. In her defense, while Dora Bell went to school in Milltown many years ago, she had not worked in town and didn't have much of a social life. Thus, she was was not acquainted with women who were known to the other volunteers. When she suggested conducting background checks on these ladies, the other volunteers managed to get her to waive the investigation. At one time, in her efforts to do a good job, she instituted an indoctrination session for new volunteers. It took her about 45 minutes to run through all the complexities of working in the shop. That program was short lived, however, as it overwhelmed the new prospects.

Usually two or three ladies worked each shift. New volunteers were always assigned to work with an experienced one. One kept track of the sales in a notebook, took the money and made change. The other(s) would bag purchases, retrieve items from the window, take pictures down from the wall, etc. It was pretty straightforward, and since most of the women had been around the block a time or two, they figured out what needed to be done pretty quickly.

A couple of Dora's other "brainstorms" didn't last long, or materialize at all, either. For instance, the orange dot system for incoming donations seemed like a good idea at first. Donations often came in numerous bags and/or boxes. Pairs, such as candlesticks, salt and pepper shakers, cream and sugar sets, socks, etc. sometimes became separated. On the rare occasion that the "assistant" Scarlet Sage, (named because of her red hair and wisdom) who claimed the role of "marker," didn't happen to get through all the bags or boxes on the same shift, mates would turn up at a later time which belonged to an item previously priced, put out for sale, and/or, heaven forbid, sold already. So Dora came up with this system of sticking an orange dot with a matching number on each container donated by a patron in an effort to keep a donor's items together. A chart was tacked to the bulletin board to keep track of the numbers given to the dots, the date of issue, and so on.

Mari Gold just happened to be in the shop, changing out one of the windows, the day Dora Bell dropped by with her new bright idea. Dora made her first stop directly inside the shop at the window where Mari Gold was establishing a theme concurrent with the closest holiday. Dora launched into an explanation which lasted a good 15 or 20 minutes. When she realized that she had lost Mari Gold's attention, she proceeded into the back room to go through the whole idea again with the other volunteers working that day.

"Wow, she didn't even come up for air!" Eddie the Trivia Guy exclaimed. He had been wandering about the shop during the dissertation and was amazed at what he had just witnessed.

Dora visited the shop every shift that week to explain the

orange dot system. It worked for awhile, but eventually the dots were left unapplied to donations.

Another time, Dora brought in a computerized cash register, in an effort to make tallying up sales easier. The shop did not have a cash register, or a computer. All sales were itemized in a notebook with a description of the item, price and tax listed in separate columns. It was rather tedious for the person keeping track of the sales, and for the customers.

Dora brought in a gentleman to show the ladies how to use the new fandangled cash register. Electronics of any kind simply frightened most of the ladies. After just a couple of lessons, the cash register ended up on a shelf in the back room with a "Do Not Touch" sign attached. Scarlet worried about the amount of electricity it was using, since it remained plugged in. The plug was pulled and another of Dora's brainstorms went unfulfilled.

A regular at the shop was a fellow Mari Gold dubbed "Jack Backpack." He always had a backpack into which he placed his purchases, usually some gadget or a book. He often could be seen walking up and down Main Street. This man was paranoid and at times interfered when he thought a customer was trying to get an item for less than the marked price. On one such occasion, a woman trying to bargain down the price of a piece of jewelry, was told by Jack, rather belligerently, to pay up and not expect to get something for nothing. Mari Gold asked him to be quiet and told the customer that he didn't work there.

The next week, Dora Bell came up with the idea that the volunteers needed to wear name tags, so people could differentiate between the workers and customers who might be taken for a volunteer. She printed up a name tag for each "volunteer," and provided cute stickers for them to decorate their tags. The name tags were then placed in a plastic holder and attached to a neckband. The ladies wore their name tags for a few months, but eventually most of them just didn't bother.

One thing for sure. Dora Bell deserved an "A" for effort. She tried hard and never seemed to get discouraged even when she found herself up against some pretty strong-willed and opinionated women. Despite that fact, and her handicaps, she carried on willingly as Chairman.

The Assistant

Then there was the assistant chairman, Scarlet Sage. She and Dora Bell never saw eye to eye and avoided working the same shift. In her mid-80's, she was still going strong. She colored her curly locks a bright red for many years, but following a lengthy illness, she decided to go "au naturel." She often wore clothes and jewelry which she purchased at the shop, and when a holiday was near, she dressed for it. She wore a witch's costume at Halloween, and for several years, a Santa suit at Christmas.

She suffered with hip problems, which lead to surgery, taking her out of the shop for a few months. At times she used a walker. She also had eye problems and had to endure some sort of injections. Occasionally, she suffered with dizzy spells and couldn't drive. But these minor inconveniences never stopped her. Truly dedicated, she showed up religiously at her command post to price all the incoming donations, with the exception of clothes, purses, books, magazines, CDs, VHS tapes and the like, which had set prices. She was the only volunteer who claimed a desk and taped her name to various supplies.

Scarlet Sage stayed until every last kitchen utensil or small appliance, glassware, artwork, candlestick, knick knack, lamp, or piece of jewelry was priced and ready to go out to the front of the shop. She was quite knowledgeable, and thereby assumed the position as the official "marker." She often took bags of jewelry home to price, and broken items to repair.

Mari Gold asked Scarlet on numerous occasions why she wouldn't accept help with the job of pricing, telling her that she shouldn't let herself become overburdened when there were tons of donations. Mari Gold hammered on saying that it wasn't a paid job, etc., but she'd get nowhere. When Scarlet first assumed the role, she brought her granddaughter in to help, but eventually the kid went off to college. A couple of other volunteers, who acted as her legs, as she put it, helped for awhile. They would find a place for the newly priced items, or set them on a "To Be Put Out" table. These women all eventually left, some due to illness, others just faded into the unknown.

For years, a group of women met on Monday mornings to sort and price the donations. That way there could be a consensus as to the value of the items. When Scarlet assumed the sole responsibility, other volunteers questioned her opinion as to the value of items, saying that some things were priced too high or too low. Scarlet, however, continued on as the volunteer with the responsibility of pricing.

Once in awhile, if a customer dealt in used goods, either at flea markets, church fairs or such, she, or he, would suggest that certain items were worth more than the shop was asking for them. Of course, the opinion of most of the volunteers was that the items were donated to begin with and that the shop couldn't expect to get what an item might fetch elsewhere.

Scarlet was a real stickler for rules and often quoted "the

law." Shortly after Mari Gold began working at the shop, she found three or four wooden canes in the trash. Seeing nothing wrong with the canes, she retrieved them, priced them and put them out for sale. The next time she came to the shop, the canes were back in the trash. So, once again she put them out. When she found them in the trash a third time, she inquired as to why perfectly good canes were being disposed of. Scarlet proclaimed that "it was against the law to sell wooden canes." Mari Gold then asked "why on earth" are they sold in every other thrift or consignment shop. Scarlet stood her ground, stating that wooden canes could break which could be grounds for a law suit. Mari Gold opined that was ridiculous, but the canes ended up in the trash.

Shortly after Mari Gold took over decorating the windows, she had created an Easter window which she was quite proud of. Lots of stuffed bunnies were part of her display. A day or so later she stopped by the shop to discover that all the bunnies had been tossed in a heap in the back room. She asked why. She also noticed that the few children's clothes that had been out for sale were gone. She was informed by Scarlet that "the State" had sent a letter noting a new law which said thrift shops could not sell children's items because they could contain lead. Scarlet warned that the State would be checking on the shop to make sure it was complying with the law.

Mari Gold didn't understand how there could be lead in clothes. Apparently buttons, zippers, etc. might be culprits. She was dumbfounded to think that children's books were suspect, for Pete's sake. She mumbled to herself that she doubted seriously that the authorities would be wasting time checking up on a tiny thrift shop. But she let it go, thinking "heaven forbid the shop gets in trouble for breaking the law."

A sign posted on the door of the shop instructed that donations not be left in the doorway when the shop was closed. But donations were left anyway, sometimes containing children's items which had to be discarded. Over time, dolls, teddy bears, beanie babies, etc., were kept because grown women collect these things.

The Donations

When Mari Gold first came on board, she noticed that an awful lot of donated stuff was being thrown out without being given a chance to sell. She inquired why this was and was told that if a donation was deemed to have absolutely no value, it was thrown away. Mari Gold tried to educate those doing the tossing that "one woman's trash is another's treasure."

Mari Gold always thought of herself as the Queen of Thrift. Being one-eighth Scotch-Irish (apparently leaning more to the Scotch) she had been recycling, repurposing and reusing things long before most people. She hated to see anything go to waste, but had to admit that some donations really did belong in the trash. Paying to dispose of other people's trash, however, didn't make sense, especially since the shop was in existence to raise money for the local hospital.

Apparently this had been a problem for years. A framed newspaper article featuring the shop in 2002 hung in the back room. It pictured a former chairwoman who reportedly posted a sign: "The Thrift Shop is not a substitute for the town dump!"

Don't know what happened to that sign, not that it would have done any good to post it.

Volunteers were asked from time to time to look over items being donated, and not to just blindly accept anything that was dropped off. Some of the ladies did not feel comfortable saying no to whatever was being donated. Some felt that it would discourage people from donating at all. Dora Bell, for one, generally accepted any donation with great enthusiasm, and greeted people donating small plastic grocery bags as if they were valuable commodities.

Mari Gold thought one of the greatest repurposing ideas that had caught on in recent years, obviously introduced by some genius woman, was to knit or crochet the small plastic bags into hand and tote bags. Amazing. A new craft idea was born for seniors to entertain themselves at their local centers.

Mari Gold suggested that the volunteers at the shop just use common sense when accepting donations, and be tactful when turning down items which could not in good conscience be put out for sale. "You don't have to get nasty," she noted. It was ridiculous, she'd say, to accept stained bed linens, or clothes that were dirty or torn.

Donations of this sort were dropped at the door when the shop was closed, despite the posted sign. Bags and boxes left outside sometimes were rummaged through with discarded items strewn about in the doorway or on the sidewalk. There didn't seem to be a remedy for this annoying situation, short of posting an armed guard at the door when the shop was closed. That wasn't going to happen. At one time a "Police Take Notice," sign was posted, but that didn't do any good either. "People don't pay any attention to signs," Mari Gold insisted.

After town-wide yard sales, the shop would be swamped

with the leftovers. One year it looked as though someone had cleaned out a kid's summer camp with the remnants finding their way into the back room of the shop. Sheets and comforters, some smelly and dirty, were stuffed into big plastic tubs. Bins containing crayons, books with their pages torn or turned up, itsy bitsy toys, and all sorts of miscellanea were overflowing. It took days to plow through the mountains of donations.

One day a regular customer who worked at another thrift-type store, overheard a conversation about what to do with unwanted donations or items that weren't selling. She said that their shop used a man who ran a business buying up clothes and all sorts of textiles which he shipped to other countries. Mari Gold asked the woman if she had this guy's number. The customer said she didn't have it with her but would bring it in on her next visit.

Mari Gold was quite excited at this prospect and shared it with other volunteers. Once she had the number, Mari Gold dialed him up and arrangements were made to have him come by the shop. The "back room" ladies were ecstatic over this find. They referred to him as the "ragman." He was a Godsend, actually paying by the pound for clothing, bed linens, cloth suitcases, and other like items which had until then been put in the trash for pickup. Scarlet kept a notebook listing the check amount received and made sure those checks came in following each pickup.

The ragman also supplied the name of a woman who took glassware, like old fashioned champagne glasses, odd wine glasses, candy dishes and the like — items which invariably took up valuable shelf space for months. That source was short lived, however.

There was a successful exchange for a year or two with

the ragman, but then the shop stopped receiving checks, the pickups ceased, and he wasn't answering his phone or returning messages. Word was he went to work for someone else in another area and was no longer available. The ladies sobbed for months over the loss of the ragman!

The Wednesday Morning Crew

Scarlet routinely worked Wednesday mornings and claimed for several years that their crew was the best, had the most fun, etc. even though it would be difficult for her to actually know how much or how little fun other volunteers were having on their shifts.

For awhile she seemed to have a group of admirers and followers who swarmed around her desk beckoning to her every call. She would cater to "special" customers for whom she saved items she thought they'd be interested in buying.

One such person was Big Mike, who made it a point to drop in on Wednesday mornings. He bragged about being a ladies man. Standing a good 6'4" and probably weighing at least 350 pounds, upon entering, he'd say, "It's okay ladies, no need to stand," or some similar bit of obnoxiousness. It was all in fun though. He was a charmer, for sure, even with a skunk white stripe running through his thick, wild black hair.

Mike worked at flea markets and was always on the lookout for something he could make a buck on. Every time he picked up an item, no matter what the price, he'd say, "Gee, only 25 cents, what a bargain." He often bought lingerie for his lady friends, and sometimes showed off pictures of himself surrounded by his girl friends at the beach or in a pool.

On one of his weekly visits, he wore a large black leather jacket adorned with pins, patches and various other interesting attachments. It was quite the display.

"We should call the newspaper," Shammy O'Rock exclaimed. So Mari Gold, who had worked for the local newspaper years before, called and asked if they could send over a photographer. The gal who showed up to take a picture expressed genuine amazement over the jacket, but no one ever spotted a photo of it in the paper.

Shammy, affectionately referred to Scarlet as the "witch." She got away with it because, at Scarlet's command, Shammy defrosted the refrigerator using a hair dryer, mopped the floors, cleaned the bathroom, washed dishes and polished silver even when she was hooked up to an oxygen tank! Shammy was one hundred percent Irish, brogue and all. Her quick wit kept the staff and customers laughing.

Then there was Susie Black. She wore her short black hair in a spiked style, although her eyes weren't black, but dark brown. "She's my legs," Scarlet would say, especially when her legs weren't working well. Susie took priced items out front with orders from Scarlet to find a place for them. She didn't quite have the knack for how or where to best display things. She just plopped items on top of other things, or wherever she could find a spot. She aimed to please, however. Susie made popcorn in the microwave if Scarlet was hungry, or ran next door to the Subway for a pizza or sandwich.

Hazel Whisp worked the counter on Wednesday mornings.

She wore about a size 2, and was always dressed neat as a pin, every hair in place, and nails professionally polished. She manned the counter pretty much singlehandedly, writing up the sales, then wrapping glassware or folding clothes meticulously, before bagging them. When the store wasn't busy, Hazel buzzed around with the vacuum cleaner. (Remember the old t.v. show where the maid's name was Hazel?)

The year the hospital was celebrating its 125th anniversary, tickets were being sold for a Christmas-in-July show at the local historic theater just across the street from the Thrift Shop. Mari Gold stopped by to check on the ticket sales and noticed that Hazel had her hands full at the front counter with customers trying to beat her down on the prices. Shammy was joking around with one of the customers and Susie was asking, "Who wants popcorn."

While dealing with the bargaining customer and trying to wrap up a tea set for another customer, Hazel asked Mari Gold if she could look for a box to put it in. As soon as Mari Gold entered the back room, Scarlet tried to enlist her help with a large box which she wanted placed up on a shelf. Mari Gold told her she'd be with her in a minute but needed to help Hazel. Having found a suitable container, Mari Gold returned to the front counter. By then, three or four more customers had lined up to make purchases, so she stayed put to help Hazel, thus dodging the heavy lifting.

It was a common occurrence for several people to pile things on the counter to purchase at the same time. It usually was simultaneous with a customer wanting to look at the jewelry displayed under the glass at that counter. Mari Gold always got frustrated with people who wouldn't wait in line like they would have to everywhere else!

Many times one or more of these customers did not, or claimed not to, speak English. Invariably, they were the ones trying to beat the ladies down on the price, insisting that a $2 item be sold for "one dollar." This exchange continued until the customer ultimately agreed to pay the $2. Mari Gold usually did not have the patience of her fellow volunteers. When she was working and this happened she was known to tell the customer, "Either pay the price, or put it back. This isn't a flea market! We're here to raise money for the Hospital."

At some point, Hazel and Mari Gold began working Saturday mornings, since the ladies who worked Saturdays for years chose to retire. There was a shortage of volunteers, so Hazel and Mari Gold agreed to take every other Saturday.

One such Saturday—although this sort of thing happened every day of the week—several customers came in all at once. A gentleman and his adult son were purchasing items individually, creating two piles on the counter. A different family of four began piling things up also. After paying for their purchases, the father and son made another sweep of the shop and found more to buy. Meanwhile, other customers came to the counter with their purchases, but the men felt they had been there first and tried cutting in front of the others. At time like this, it's quite the challenge keeping track of who is buying what. Hazel always handled these situations like a pro while Mari Gold mumbled obscenities under her breath.

The Clothes Lady

The shop received bags of clothes, not little bags, but trashsized bags. Many of the volunteers brought their used clothes to the shop on a regular basis. Heaps of clothes were donated to the shop by family members cleaning out the home of a loved one who had passed. Often it was that of a former volunteer. There was never a shortage. Mari Gold would say that by the time she cleaned out her closet, her clothes were ready for the rag bag. No one would want them. Some donations fell into that category but people brought them in anyway.

Hosta LaSeeya was the clothes handler — named for her favorite plant, which propagates like the clothes did in the shop. She had given several off-spring to Mari Gold, who then had more of the plants than she could find places for in her yard, not unlike the clothes for which there was no room in the shop. When Hosta was ready to leave for the day, she had the habit of saying, "See yah when I see yah."

She was a truly dedicated volunteer. She worked with the Wednesday crew, but preferred to stay in the back room rather than deal directly with the customers at the counter. She was always congenial to the customers, however. She often worked when the shop was closed to take advantage of the absence of distraction. Hosta plowed through bags and piles of the donated clothing, sorting men's from the women's, spring and summer from fall and winter, a daunting task to say the least. After items were sorted, and the out-of-season articles packed away, clothes that she deemed suitable for sale were placed on the "ready-to-go-out" rack.

Even though the volunteers were instructed to only put out items which had been priced, or clothing from the "ready-to-go-out" rack, many times the ladies would get rambunctious and put out newly donated clothing which had not been subjected to Hosta's quality control. Hosta would get her leaves in a flutter when she found turtlenecks hanging on her racks. She'd claim that she couldn't remember the last time a turtleneck sold. Mari Gold would think to herself, "Gee, I still wear them."

One of Hosta's pet peeves was finding clothes hanging on the wrong rack, or hangers going the wrong way. Hangers were often the subject of discussion. One volunteer used to remark, "I don't know who the idiot is who hangs blouses on hangers meant for skirts." This woman eventually quit because she didn't agree with having to pay the $5.00 required. (Volunteers had to be dues-paying members of the Guild in order to work in the shop.)

Hangers accumulated in the back room, remarkably, because clothes usually did not come in on them. Only plastic or wood hangers were used. Never wire. One might recall a movie in which Joan Crawford went off on her daughter like she had committed a capital offense for using wire hangers. Apparently, many of the volunteers felt the same way about them. When there was an over-abundance of plastic and wood hangers, they were tied together and sold 10 for a dollar. Amazingly, they sold very well. Wire hangers, however, went straight in the trash.

Sometimes there would be a special rack for better brands or "designer labels." Other times there just weren't enough of these better brands to warrant a separate rack. Hosta usually was against higher prices, saying that "people love shops like ours where they can find a real treasure."

Invariably though, a discussion would ensue that it didn't seem right that a woman's blouse from an inexpensive outlet should sell for the same price as one from a "high end" store. Pretty expensive things would end up selling for an outrageous bargain. Violet (who will be introduced later) told Mari Gold at least a hundred times about how she and Dominique (a former chairman) had a special "boutique" rack for the better brands. "Everything was hung on black hangers. The customers would go right to that rack when they came in," she'd say.

When it was decided there were enough "designer labels" to warrant a separate rack, a special price tag was attached. So if a customer removed the price tag in order to only be charged the regular price, a plastic pull-through was evidence that the tag had been removed.

There was an occasion when the shop received several bags of an exclusive line of clothing which was only available through home parties. A couple of the volunteers practically swooned when they saw this special line of skirts, tops and dresses. The dollar rack was cleared of clothing which had been hanging around, and the new donations, with their tags still attached, were placed on it, noting the brand, the retail price, and the shop's price.

For the next couple of days, it was like the shop turned

into Filene's Basement. Women flocked to the rack and bought the new line like it was being given away. Best of all, no one squawked about the prices! One day, several Louis Vuitton handbags were donated. The volunteers working that day did not recognize the name and placed the handbags out among all the other "mongrel" bags. Needless to say, some lucky bargain hunter, or dealer, hit "pay dirt,"only paying the $2.00 price of an ordinary handbag.

Hosta preferred to work on Monday afternoons when the shop was closed. Mari Gold also preferred changing out the windows on Monday afternoons, rather than when customers were underfoot. In previous years when the shop was closed all day Monday "for inventory," several ladies came in to dust, vacuum, rearrange, wash glassware, remove items which hadn't sold in months, and so forth. At some point, Dora decided that the shop should be open Monday mornings since a crew was there working anyway. That's when Hosta and Mari Gold started coming in Monday afternoons.

When Hosta had the clothes organized, removing things that had not sold, or changing over for the upcoming season and Mari Gold was satisfied with the looks of her windows, they'd do a little housecleaning and canvas the shop for items collecting dust.

"This has been here since Hector was a pup," Hosta would remark about something she thought had been around for too long. She'd toss the item into a trash bag. Mari Gold, who felt everything would sell eventually, tried to convince her that the item hadn't been around all that long. "Let's give it another week or so," she'd suggest. Sometimes Hosta would concede but other times the item would be tossed.

Hosta was the Queen of Quotes for sure, often spouting off quirky sayings in response to Mari Gold's actions. When Mari Gold became sidetracked, as often was the case, going from one thing to another, Hosta would say, "One thing done and done well." At some point, Mari Gold looked up quotations and found a famous one attributed to Plato. It goes, "Better a little that is well done than a great deal imperfectly." That was most likely the root of Hosta's quote.

"A cup is a cup is a cup," Hosta insisted when she'd find a cup or mug marked more than ten cents. Mari Gold tried to convince her that there was a difference between a cup or mug mass produced for a bank or institution as opposed to one from an exotic place or one painted by an artist, or just a pretty mug from a gift shop which originally sold for as much as $10 — certainly worth more than a dime. Hosta would stick to her opinion, saying "Let's just agree to disagree."

One summer when Mari Gold was painting a large counter with some paint she had on hand, she mentioned that the color had a tinge of purple. "It looks white to me," Hosta opined.

"Really, you can't you see the hint of pinkish purple? Look at the dried paint on the can's label," Mari Gold pressed. "No, still looks white to me," Hosta insisted, stating "A man convinced against his will is of the same opinion." Mari Gold finally gave up.

Hosta LaSeeya was what some would consider a minimalist. She hated when the shop became cluttered. Mari Gold wondered what on earth attracted Hosta to the shop in the first place if she was bothered by clutter. "What's a thrift shop without clutter," she said to herself. Mari Gold had a habit of retrieving things Hosta tossed into the trash bin, feeling sure the particular item would sell. When it did, she invariably informed her co-volunteer about the sale. "Amazing," Hosta would remark.

Mari Gold often told her friend that they'd never be able to live together. Hosta agreed. But the two of them worked well together and became good friends.

As stated earlier, when they had enough of the shop, Hosta would say, "See yah when I see yah," usually adding something to the effect that she could hear the ice cubes rattling in the glass. One thing the two women agreed on was cocktail hour, or more specifically, martinis, although Hosta preferred Tangurey to Mari Gold's taste for Absolut!

The Little Italian Lady

"What is it with these Italian women?" Mari Gold often thought to herself.

Mari Gold was at the shop alone one afternoon setting up one of the windows. An old time customer came by who was known to Mari Gold because she had also frequented the wallpaper and paint store where Mari Gold worked before retiring. She mouthed that the store was closed and that she was just changing out the windows.

"I come-a-by three times. You closed," Mrs. Leone said. "I dont-a always have-a ride." She remained outside and kept talking. Mari Gold finally gave up and let her in, telling her she'd give her a couple of minutes to look around but that she was trying to get the windows done.

Mrs. Leone was only about four feet ten, had short very curly salt and pepper hair, and always wore a house dress. (For those who don't know what a house dress is, it's a simple, usually small floral print dress worn by elderly Italian women.)

Mari Gold climbed back into the window, only to have Mrs. Leone ask to see a doll which was up on a shelf. As she reached for the doll, a couple of other dolls fell to the floor. "How-a-much," Mrs. Leone asked. "Fifteen dollars," Mari Gold replied. "Too much. I don't-a- have that-a-much money." Mari Gold said "sorry" and returned the dolls to their place, then stepped back into the window, using her trusty step stool.

"How-amuch that basket?" the little woman asked. "It's a dollar," Mari Gold told her, "but the utensils, napkins and plates are an additional dollar." Mrs. Leone scrunched up her face and made a noise to indicate that she didn't like the price. "Oh, just leave a dollar on the counter," Mari Gold said in exasperation.

"Do you have-a phone I can-a use. I need to call some-abody for a ride," Mrs. Leone asked next. Becoming annoyed, Mari Gold stepped back out of the window and went to get the phone for her. Mrs. Leone proceeded to dial but needed assistance. "No ringing." Mari Gold took the phone and pressed the call button and handed it back to her. "No-a-body home. I have-a-nother number." When there was no answer at the second number, she bent herself in half and reached down deep into her bag which was on the floor. "I have-a-one-amore number." After another minute or so, she announced, "No answer there-a either. I need-a ride home."

Just then a woman known to Mari Gold knocked on the window. Mari Gold unlocked the door to tell her the shop was closed and asked if she could possibly give Mrs. Leone a ride home. The woman asked where Mrs. Leone lived, but upon hearing the address, said she didn't go that way.

"Come on, I'll give you a ride home," Mari Gold said, adding, "I'm done with the window for now anyway."

Violet

Mari Gold started working with Violet on Thursday mornings after her "training period" with Rosie was up. She was Italian, like Rosie, and was originally from New York. Violet (named after this little flower because at 90 she was shrinking, although only in size) was still quite attractive, with beautiful thick, mostly gray, but not white hair. She told Mari Gold she cut it herself and could not remember the last time she'd been to a hairdresser.

Violet wasn't anything like Rosie. Never saw her fingernails painted. She wore very little jewelry, just simple little gold earrings and a small cross around her neck. She mostly wore navy blue or brown. She didn't swear or tell off-color jokes.

She was soft spoken and, as noted, rather small in stature. In fact, she was so tiny that one day when it was snowing, she wanted to move her car. Mari Gold offered to do it for her, but the driver's seat was moved up so close to the steering wheel that Mari Gold couldn't even get into the car.

Another tiny 90-plus-year-old who worked in the shop, mostly with Dora, was Joni Jumpup. She wore a blond wig, lots of makeup and jewelry. She loved clothes, especially anything with sequins, including shoes, wore mini skirts with nylons, and lacy or sequined blouses. She even had a boyfriend! She was a character for sure, and the customers loved her. She had worked for years in a thrift shop in Florida, where she retired. When she eventually returned to Massachusetts, she stopped into the Thrift Shop to see if volunteers were needed. Dora was working that day and was ecstatic to have a seasoned thrift shop worker to add to her ranks.

Violet had been volunteering for at least 20 years. Mari Gold asked what, or who, brought her into the shop. She told her that the former chairman, Dominique, had been a nurse at a nearby Army base, and knew that Violet was a widow of an Army veteran. The two women lived at the same condo development and had become acquainted. Dominique was looking for volunteers and thought that Violet might like to help out in the shop. Violet eventually became Dominique's co-chair.

Mari Gold told Violet that she met Dominique when she came to the wallpaper and paint store, which also sold flooring, to buy carpet for the shop. She mentioned she thought she was "a sweet lady."

"Sweet, ha. Sweet she was not! That's certainly not how I'd describe her," Violet remarked. "She was nice enough and loved running the shop, but she always delegated all the work." Violet added that Dominique did go to yard sales on weekends, however, "to buy things with her own money to help stock the place."

But when she decided to have the shop painted, Violet said Dominique ordered them all around to move racks and such out of the way, but that she "never lifted a finger."

Dominique liked to entertain and invited the volunteers to her home occasionally. At Christmas, she'd include husbands, but then she would ignore the women, Violet said, adding, "she was a big flirt." Then she said, "Don't get me wrong. We became good friends and when she died I missed her. I still do."

Whenever a gentleman entered the shop wearing a Veteran's cap, Violet would ask which branch of service he had served in, even though it most likely was evident on the cap he wore. That usually started a conversation, but sometimes ignited a string of war stories which lasted a lot longer than Violet had bargained for. Mari Gold would busy herself around the shop, figuring at least Violet had someone to talk to.

One gentleman commented that he had just gotten hearing aides through the Veterans Hospital. He said he hadn't heard his own voice in years. His wife chimed in, "or mine." He related how the men were never supplied protection of any kind for their ears and that they experienced terrible ringing in their ears from gunfire. "Some of the guys' ears actually bled," he added.

He talked on and on. Afterwards, Violet said to Mari Gold, "Thanks a lot for just leaving me here alone with that man," but Mari Gold thought she was giving Violet "something to do." Violet often asked what she could do to help when Mari Gold buzzed around the shop. But she was unsteady on her feet because of bad knees. Mari Gold would tell her just to stay put and "man the book."

Over the years, Violet became forgetful. She'd tell Mari Gold many times about the years she lived in France and Germany. She also lived in North Dakota and Virginia.

Most Thursdays Mari Gold brought coffee from home for herself and Violet, who invariably would say, "You don't have to do that. You're spoiling me." Mari Gold would say it was no trouble, that she made coffee for herself most mornings anyway. On numerous occasions Violet related to Mari Gold how she learned to drink her coffee black. When she lived in North Dakota, "people there drank so much coffee. They thought nothing of inviting you over at 9 o'clock at night for a cup of coffee." She said she started eliminating the use of sugar and cream to avoid gaining weight.

Violet was hard of hearing, and on occasion would forget to put in her hearing aides. She became flustered when more than one customer came to the counter to pay for their items at the same time, often asking more than once what the customer was purchasing. She kept track of the sales, which were individually written in a book by description, listing the price of the item, with the tax recorded in a separate column. She began having trouble remembering which sales had been written down, which ones had been paid for, if the customer had gotten their change, and so forth. She usually added up the columns several times during the shift to make sure the sheet tallied to the penny.

It became a challenge working with her, but she still wanted to come every Thursday. She had taken a bad fall one winter, breaking a hip and messing up one of her wrists. She had to take a long break from volunteering.

The winter of 2014-2015 was a particularly brutal one. The store was closed a lot that year because of enormous amounts of snow or frigid temperatures but also due to illness of the volunteers. A few of the ladies took bad falls, like Violet. One fell down her cellar stairs, broke her pelvis and several bones. Another slipped on ice and dislocated her shoulder. Still another broke her foot. And, sadly, a couple of the ladies passed away.

When Violet had recuperated from her fall, she wanted very much to return to the shop. Having become housebound when her doctor instructed her not to drive her car, she needed a ride.

It was during Violet's time away that Mari Gold began working with Butter Kupp (who had blond hair and wore yellow a lot). When Violet returned, Butter Kupp would pick her up and Mari Gold would take her home.

Mari Gold was glad to have help for Violet to keep the sales straight, although Butter Kupp always said she was "terrible with money" and that she shouldn't be allowed near it. She was very patient and would repeat to Violet as often as necessary what exactly each customer was buying and how much it cost. Then she would bag the purchases. When the customers were taken care of, she'd put out items which had been priced.

One of Violet's pet peeves was finding an item priced 75 cents or $1.25. This always lead to the story of a class she had taken on pricing. She was taught that if something was worth 75 cents, it was worth $1.00. Seventy-five cents was not a good number to use. The same thing applied to a $1.25. Either mark it $1.00 or mark it up to $1.50. This method was considered a better marketing strategy.

Like so many of the ladies who volunteer, Violet had some pretty strong opinions about how the shop should be run. She did not agree that customers should be allowed to lay merchandise aside to pick up at a later time, either that day or another, because they didn't have the money right then. "We never allowed that," she'd say to Mari Gold who would tell her that it was okay, that the customer was a regular and surely would be back with the money.

She also said many times that she "hated" to see any item

displayed in plastic. Mari Gold agreed with her about the plastic, especially when displayed in the window, but would say, "hate is a pretty strong word, Violet." "Well, I feel pretty strongly about it," Violet retorted.

Violet often mentioned how she and Dominique had a "boutique corner" for all the better brands of clothes. "We hung everything on black hangers, never metal ones. Customers just flocked to that corner. I don't know why we did away with it." While Mari Gold would say she agreed with Violet, she didn't feel that most of the time there were enough "designer" labels to warrant an exclusive rack, especially since space was so limited in the small shop.

When the morning shift was over, Violet would often ask if Mari Gold and Butter Kupp would like to go to lunch. She enjoyed treating them as a thank you for picking her up and taking her home. Butter Kupp usually was off to watch her grandbabies, but Mari Gold would take her up on the offer most of the time.

The Afternoon Shift

Thursday afternoons saw a series of volunteers, unlike other shifts which had the same ladies for years. Several years after Mari Gold began working Thursday mornings, two new ladies started covering the afternoons. First came Sweet Alyssa. She was very easy-going and soft-spoken. Best of all, she undertook, on her own, the huge responsibility of organizing the stacks of books, video tapes, CD's and DVD's which were donated by the box load. Alyssa went through the books one at a time, dusting them off, turning them upside down and flipping through the pages. Mari Gold asked if she ever found money. She said she found a $25 gift certificate to Starbucks once, and had come across "a couple of steamy notes."

Alyssa categorized the books according to romance, mystery, inspirational, gardening, cooking, etc., labeling the shelves accordingly. It was so much easier for customers to find what they were looking for. Book sales definitely increased as a result of her efforts.

At first, Alyssa went through a string of co-workers. "I guess no one wants to work with me," she joked. Nothing could have been further from the truth, as she was probably one of the easiest volunteers to work with.

A year or so later, Lu Pine (this flower being described as beautiful and on a tall spike) joined the brigade of volunteers. She was a gal who identified with Mari Gold inasmuch as she saw the "value" in what others considered trash. Her first stop each Thursday afternoon, upon entering the back room, was to check the trash and recycle bins.

Lu brought in treasurers she found at a nearby recycle center. She also took time at home to look on the internet for the going price of donated items that she thought could be valuable. She checked on everything from jewelry to Pyrex bowls to knick knacks.

She'd write a note to identify a "collectible," including what it was being sold for on eBay or Etsy. Sometimes Mari Gold looked things up, but mostly Lu did it. The two ladies enjoyed checking things out to see what they were worth. Of course, the Thrift Shop price would only be a fraction of what the item would bring on line.

The Irregulars

Maybe the fact that the Thrift Shop was located on the Main Street was the reason that it drew the local "street people." These people weren't exactly homeless, but they roamed the street trying to fill their days. It was evident that they were lonesome and sometimes just needed a place to go or someone to talk to. Most of the volunteers were sympathetic.

One fellow Mari Gold called "Jack Backpack," or "Walks with Backpack." (Mari Gold liked using Native American names. One Halloween, she dressed as a Native American woman. Her name tag identified her as "Stands with Hammer," due to the fact that she often was seen with a hammer and nails.) Jack always wore a backpack, using it to store his purchases — usually a gadget of some sort, a small electronic, a jar of nuts and bolts, or a book.

Jack Backpack was tall and thin, wore a medium length beard and a baseball cap overall usually longish hair. He had mental issues, evident by the statements he'd make.

"The thieves are out there," he'd say as he entered the store. He'd warn: "You guys better be careful. Did they already come in here and buy up all the new stuff?" If Mari Gold was on duty she'd tell him there was "nothing new" in the shop. He'd continue, however, with something like: "You know what I mean, all the new stuff you just put out. They buy up everything, then sell it on the Internet." She would tell him there wasn't anything to be done about what customers did after they purchased things.

"They come right into your yard and steal stuff," he would rant. "They're out there on the street just ready to rob you blind."

On another visit, he warned: "You guys should have a code on everything and have someone in the back room entering it in the computer, so you can keep track of what the thieves are buying up." He'd be told there was no computer in the store, that most of the volunteers were old and didn't know how to use one. Besides, the volunteers weren't interested in going to all that trouble.

He'd ask, "where's the gold?" or "got any diamonds?" Mari Gold would tell him that most people were aware of whether they had gold or silver, or precious stones, and would not be donating valuable jewelry to the shop.

The ladies heard many times about his family members who kicked him down stairs, robbed him, and so forth. He'd often say things like, "someone tried to attack me in a stairwell last night." He was asked if he called the police when things like that happened. He'd reply, "They don't do anything. In fact, one time the police kicked me when I was down on the sidewalk having a seizure."

Another story involved a trip to the hospital. During his visit he claimed, "they stole the gold out of my teeth." The tale went on that "when they were getting ready to cut me open, I grabbed my clothes and got the hell out of there."

The ladies generally let him air his grievances, although sometimes it became necessary to ask him to cool it, like when he'd ask, "Do you have any knives?" He'd be told that the shop didn't sell them. Mari Gold would be inclined to tell him that even if they did, they wouldn't be able to sell him anything that could be construed as a dangerous weapon.

"How about guns," he'd ask on another visit. "I need to be able to protect myself from all the hooligans out there." Again, he'd be asked in a diplomatic manner to knock it off. Or he might ask "How's the President doing today. Is he taking care of the illegal aliens from Mars who are taking advantage of our country, living off all the taxpayer's dollars." If the volunteer of the day gave him any attention, or engaged in his ramblings in any way, they would soon regret it.

Some days he would be in a better frame of mind. He'd say, "thank you for being open today," or "there should be more places like this shop where a person feels welcome." He'd even joke around a little. Sometimes he mentioned his mother, saying that she lived in Germany, and it saddened him that he could not visit her because he wasn't able to fly due to his seizures.

Anytime Mari Gold encountered this man on the street, she'd say "hello," but he would not respond. He simply walked on with his head down.

One thing that was different about the Thrift Shop than any other type of store was that people visited with each other while they shopped. Of course, some just looked around and brought their purchases to the counter without a lot of gab, but others hung around sharing life experiences, both happy and sad. Oftentimes customers chimed in on conversations. Women who had lost a husband or a child would share their stories. And the volunteers, being mostly older ladies, would listen and share stories too.

The volunteers were sympathetic to a local well-dressed woman, who Mari Gold referred to as Waltzing Matilda. Any day of the week, she could be observed walking up and down Main Street. Known to have had mental issues for years, she was very polite and friendly on good days, addressing the volunteers who she knew by name, always calling them "Mrs." so and so. She knew them from working in the local public school system. Other times she seemed to be off in her own world and basically non-communicative.

Matilda was probably in her 50's. She wore her hair long and often in a Victorian-type updo. She was quite stylish, had a slim figure, and enjoyed shopping for clothes. She'd hold up a blouse and a skirt or a pair of slacks and a jacket. "How does this look?" she would ask. If she was given the thumbs up, she'd ask if she could try the clothes on. After doing so, she would step out to the front of the shop, modeling her outfit, looking for opinions of volunteers and other customers. She seemed to need approval before deciding to buy her new outfits. Sometimes, she'd want the clothes held for her, which was against the store's practice, but most of the ladies would agree to set them aside.

Since the dressing room was located in the back of the shop where all donations, including clothes, were collected, volunteers were instructed to keep an eye on her since she had been known to shoplift. Unfortunately, after being observed walking out of the shop without paying for things on several occasions, she was told she would not be allowed to come into the shop any longer.

Matilda continued to come around nonetheless. She'd peer in the windows, a cup of coffee in hand, or just hang around the doorway. She'd often point to something she wanted to see. Some of the volunteers felt bad for her and would bring things to the door, but others told her she wasn't allowed inside to buy the item. She also had the habit of talking to incoming customers, giving them the impression that she worked at the shop as a type of greeter.

Another man Mari Gold referred to as "the Poor Soul" had obvious mental problems. He wandered the streets talking to no one in particular, and had been observed carrying on a full-blown conversation while dining alone at a local restaurant. He'd wait at the door in the morning before the shop opened. If the door wasn't unlocked right at 10 o'clock, he'd keep tapping his watch, saying, "It's ten o'clock. They're supposed to be open. It's 10 o'clock." Tap, tap, tap. "When the sign says open at 10 o'clock, the door should not be locked." He'd go on until the door was unlocked.

He would wander around the shop talking to himself, repeating the same thing over and over. Once in awhile he would buy something like a cookie jar, stating that his mother collected them. He rambled on about any subject with which he was consumed at the time, like music from the 50's and 60's.

One day a woman, unknown to the volunteers, came inside the shop and stopped dead in her tracks just inside the door. She just stood there staring up at a collection of dolls displayed on a shelf. She pointed to them and began ranting, "Those dolls are really ugly. They really give me the creeps. They are really, really creepy." She continued for several minutes, then hurriedly exited the shop.

For several years Chatty Cathy, who had been an antiques dealer, frequented the shop. Hooked up to her oxygen tank,

Chatty would make her way to a chair which used to be available for the customers. (At some later time, the chair was removed.) Because of her knowledge of antiques and collectibles, Chatty would sit there for hours, making comments about items customers were buying. She involved herself in everyone's conversation. When she complained about being tired, Mari Gold seized the opportunity to suggest, "Why don't you go home and lie down for awhile."

"I'm sick and tired of being at home staring at the walls," Chatty would answer. She'd stay in the chair until her son or friend came by to give her a ride home.

A younger man, of slight build, who Mari Gold nicknamed "the Shuffler," visited the shop for a year or so. His head hung downward and he walked with a drag in his footstep. One of the first times he came to the shop, it was just before Christmas. He was like a kid in a toy store.

He bought an artificial tree, then announced he had no way to get it home. Hazel asked where he lived. When he said "only a couple of blocks from here," she offered to give him a ride to his apartment. Later that same day, he returned, all excited, to buy lights and ornaments for his tree. The ladies were happy to see a pour soul having some fun.

The Shuffler began to frequent the shop, always buying some little thing. One day a social worker reportedly came by and instructed that he was not allowed to buy anything due to a problem with hoarding. His picture was posted on the bulletin board in the back room with a note saying, "Don't let this man buy anything."

So every time he came into the store, the ladies, following the order, told him that they weren't allowed to sell him anything.

He became quite irritated and said he just got a new social worker. Standing there in a stew, he'd say he was moving anyway and should be allowed to buy whatever he wanted.

A few of the volunteers didn't agree with the order and over time most sold him whatever he brought to the counter, feeling sorry for him. It was generally just some little trinket he wanted. There was never a note stating that any social worker had checked back about his purchases.

This fellow became pretty much a daily visitor. He rambled on about one thing and another. He talked like he had a mouth full of marbles, which made it quite difficult to understand him. He repeatedly insisted that it was okay for him to buy things because he was moving, or had a new social worker. On one of his last visits, he asked about a set of green canisters in the window. Mari Gold told him they were $12. He said he didn't have that much money on him, but was getting a check in a couple of days. Mari Gold commented that the canisters were rather large, kind of heavy to carry. She asked if he really needed them and suggested that he come back when he had the money. This wasn't done to be unkind, just keeping in mind the hoarding accusation.

A few days later this man was in the shop browsing. Butter Kupp observed him leaving with a DVD player tucked under his arm, which he hadn't paid for. It had a price tag of $25. She immediately brought this to Mari Gold's attention, who went outside and called to him, asking him to return to the shop. He didn't offer an explanation. The matter needed to be discussed with the chairman and others, who felt it necessary to have a restraining order issued, barring him from the shop. He did not attempt to come in after that, but was often seen walking by, head hanging, wearing a shirt with some crazy print, an odd hat or comical shoes.

One day a woman shopper, who was looking through the ladies' tops, kept leaning against the rack. Blouses and sweaters kept falling off the hangers, and she apologized, saying she wasn't able to bend over to pick them up. She was told it was okay, that the volunteers would take care of it. After purchasing several tops, she asked about a Congregational church which she thought was on the corner. Mari Gold told her the only church nearby was Catholic. The woman then started talking, but was not making sense. Mari Gold said she was sorry but she didn't understand her. She finally decided to leave.

Just as she left the shop, another customer approached Mari Gold and told her she thought the woman was dehydrated and could pass out. She told Mari Gold she should call the non-emergency police number. Although she was busy with other customers, Mari Gold grabbed the phone book. Unable to quickly access the non-emergency number, she handed the book to the concerned customer to find it for her. Finally, Mari Gold dialed the number, only to get a recording. When connected to a dispatcher, she related the incident, including the woman's description. Later a police officer stopped in to inform the ladies that he had not been able to locate anyone fitting the description provided.

Afterwards, Mari Gold thought she should have told the concerned customer to chase after the woman herself, sit her down and bring her some water. "Next time," she thought.

Other Visitors

Harry was a regular. He always wore a baseball cap over long, straggly hair. He also reeked of cigarette smoke. Mari Gold nicknamed him "Dirty Harry." He pontificated about politics, religion or some other subject of controversy. It bugged him that the women who went to the gym next door parked in spaces right out in front of the gym. "Amazing" he'd say. "They're going to work out, but heaven forbid they walk any distance to and from their cars."

He was somewhat knowledgeable when it came to collectibles and preferred the unusual. He bought things like ugly banks and items the volunteers were sure no one would want.

On one of Harry's visits, Violet was talking about how she met a couple of Popes when she lived in Europe, but she couldn't remember which ones. Mari Gold asked if it could have been Pope Pius XII or Pope John XXIII, given the years she was there.

"There was a woman pope back in the 15th century," Harry piped up. Mari Gold said she didn't think there was ever a woman pope. Harry insisted there had been. "I think her name was Ignatius Loyola or something like that," Harry said, to which

Violet replied she didn't think that Ignatius was a woman's name. Harry still seemed sure of himself, but the subject was dropped.

Mari Gold decided to research Ignatius Loyola and discovered there was a Saint Ignatius who was a Spanish Basque priest from Loyola. He found the order of priests known as the Jesuits. These priests served the Pope as missionaries.

A man Mari Gold dubbed "Tricky Dick" was another regular for a few years. He liked military stuff, medals, patches, jackets and so forth. Scarlet kept a few military patches and buttons in the top drawer of her desk, but was of the opinion that it was "illegal" for the shop to sell them. So one day Mari Gold took a ride to a Army/Navy store in a nearby town. She showed the owner the items in question. According to the gentleman at the store, the items could be sold without breaking any laws. Scarlet accepted the opinion with skepticism, but wouldn't let Tricky Dick buy any of the items.

On one of his visits, Tricky Dick observed a couple of nice throws, which Scarlett had marked $20 and $25 and which had just been put out for sale. They were like new with scenes of lighthouses on them and several people commented about how nice there were.

A few days later when Mari Gold was working with Violet, Tricky Dick dropped by. Mari Gold was busy in the back with Hosta, but later asked Violet if he had bought anything. She said he had purchased "two lovely throws." Mari Gold expressed amazement, saying, "You mean to tell me he bought those throws that were marked $20! The ones with the lighthouses on them."

Violet stepped back and, with puzzlement in her voice, said that they were only marked one dollar apiece.

"What?" Mari Gold said in exasperation. "He must have

pulled the prices off and replaced them with dollar tags. He was here yesterday when they were put out and knew very well that they were marked $20 and $25!"

Most of the time prices were simply written in pen on a piece of masking tape, so it was easy enough for a customer to pull off the price they didn't like and replace it with one that they liked better.

Violet kept saying that she felt "just terrible." Upon hearing this exchange, Hosta came bounding out from the back room. "That dirtbag," she exclaimed. "You mean to tell me he conned Violet. He knew how much those things were priced," reiterating what Mari Gold had said. She asked Hosta and Violet if they thought she should call the police, stating, "he knew doggone well what price was on those throws. That's why I keep saying we need to use some other method of marking prices. It's too easy for people to just pull off the tape."

With Hosta and Violet in agreement, Mari Gold placed the phone call. Within minutes, an officer showed up and was apprised of the incident. The officer asked if the ladies knew where this guy lived. Hosta supplied the name of an apartment complex which she thought was where he lived. A short time later, however, the officer returned saying the man was not known at that address. He asked if the ladies wanted to press charges.

The consensus was "No." But Mari Gold said that she would "take care of it." She had an idea about where he was living, so she paid a visit to the Town Hall to confirm that he was holding up in a house which had a fire and was now condemned. She proceeded to write him a letter stating that the shop was aware of his shenanigans and expected him to pay the asking price for the throws, and apologize to Violet.

When Mari Gold arrived at church the next Sunday, just as she took her pew, Tricky Dick, who was an usher, approached her and asked how he could "right the situation." She told him she would speak to him after Mass. She told him then that he needed to pay for the merchandise he scammed from "poor Violet," adding that he knew what the price was and that it was pretty crummy for him to wait til she and Hosta were out of sight to pull such a stunt.

He claimed that he couldn't pay $20 each. Mari Gold told him in that case, he needed to return the throws. He said he couldn't do that because he had given them to somebody. He pleaded that he be given a break. Mari Gold told him she'd have to talk it over with the others.

After some discussion at the shop, the consensus was that $20 would be an acceptable amount for both throws, even though it amounted to less than half price. The ladies were in agreement that he should apologize to Violet. After that, he was not to return to the shop.

The next Sunday he gave Mari Gold a check for the $20. The shop did not accept checks, but this man said "believe me, there's money in the account." Being in church and all, Mari Gold took it, even though she felt strange conducting such a transaction at the back of church. The feeling passed, and as far as she knew, the check cleared.

When Mari Gold told him that he needed to apologize to Violet, he said he would not be returning to the shop. However, a week or so later, he showed up looking for military items. He made no attempt at an apology and acted as though the incident had never occurred. Mari Gold approached him, reminding him of what he had said about not returning, and that if he wasn't there to apologize, that he needed to leave. He claimed that he had never said he wouldn't come back. Mari Gold informed him that the ladies in charge planned to get a restraining order if he continued to come into the shop. He didn't return after that.

The shop was scammed another time by a young couple who called the hospital to report they had been treated in an extremely rude manner at the Thrift Shop. Hosta, who was the presiding president of the Hospital Guild, received a call about the incident. She then called Mari Gold, who had been her predecessor, to discuss how to handle the situation. It was decided that Hosta would call the customer and offer an apology, accompanied by an offer to come down to the shop and pick out something at no charge.

The young couple, dressed gothic style, complete with piercings and tattoos, came in while Mari Gold was working. They claimed that they had been treated with disrespect and that an offer of donated jewelry had been thrown back at them. Mari Gold apologized for the way they were treated, but expressed surprise that any volunteer would treat any customer in the manner they claimed. She said she understood they were to be allowed to chose something free of charge.

When the couple began picking up several items, Mari Gold became a little suspicious. So she asked them if they could describe the volunteer. They said they could, and in fact they actually had the person's picture on their phone, which they found on the internet. When they showed Mari Gold a picture of Dora, she knew something wasn't right. There was no way Dora would be rude to a customer. And upon checking the schedule, Dora had not worked that day.

Just about then Hosta came in. Mari Gold took her aside

and confided her suspicions. Hosta then told the couple they could chose one item, again offering an apology. They began to embellish their supposed "mistreatment" which only added to the puzzling situation. They finally chose a $5 item and left.

A few days later, word had spread around town that this duo had tried to pull similar stunts at other places of business.

The shop attracted lots of folks who spoke "in foreign tongues," especially Spanish and Portuguese speakers. Both men and women shopped, but it was mostly the women who came to the shop in groups of three or four. The volunteers wondered if this was done on purpose as a form of distraction. It certainly caused confusion for the keeper of the sales book.

These people loved to bargain, always asking if something marked two dollars could go for "one dollar." If it was marked five dollars, they'd want it for three or four. The volunteers repeatedly told them the prices were not negotiable. But day in and day out the same people would come to the store and ask if they could have an article for less than the marked price.

At one point, a group of the volunteers, in an effort to better communicate with Spanish-speaking customers, decided to take a Spanish class being offered at the local senior center. That helped a little, but after two years they said they were "just conjugating verbs," which wasn't helping very much. At least they were trying.

The Educators and Other Experts

First of all, there was "Jack Backpack." Almost every time he took out a dollar bill, or a five, with a twinkle in his eye, he'd ask whose picture was on the bill. Some of the ladies would guess right off, especially after being asked on numerous occasions. But once in awhile the volunteer could not remember that Washington was on the one dollar bill or Lincoln on the five. This always amused Jack so the ladies played along. He also liked to point out which state the dollar was from.

All kinds of discussions took place in the shop. One of the regulars, Mari Gold called Eddie the Trivia Guy. He'd ask questions like, "Who was the youngest President?" Everyone in the shop at the time answered "JFK."

"He was the youngest elected," Eddie informed, but Teddy Roosevelt was the youngest when he stepped in after President McKinley was assassinated.

Eddie perused the VHS tapes, telling the ladies that he held movie nights at the home where he lived. When he showed "Cat on a Hot Tin Roof," he said the women at the home loved it. Then he asked if anyone knew who was in the movie. Know-it-all

Mari Gold guessed, "Paul Newman, Elizabeth Taylor and Burl Ives." That was the right answer, Eddie announced. Then he asked, "What two movies defined Vivian Leigh's career?" Again, Mari Gold answered "Gone With the Wind was one," but she couldn't think of the other one. As soon as Eddie said it was "A Streetcar Named Desire," Mari Gold said, "I knew that."

Another time, Eddie asked which was the largest state areawise on the east coast. Mari Gold guessed Maine, but Eddie pointed out while Maine was the largest of the New England states, it was not the largest on the east coast. A couple other guesses were Florida and North Carolina. Eddie finally informed the ladies that the correct answer was Georgia. "Learn something new everyday," Mari Gold quipped.

On Saturdays, a woman, usually accompanied by her 86-year-old mother, often brought attention to items she felt were underpriced. When looking over the jewelry, she'd point out a piece of Sarah Coventry or Monet, priced at $2 or $3, and suggest that the shop should be charging at least be $5. Her visits were refreshing, given the number of customers who invariably tried to buy something for less than the asking price.

Another time she mentioned that a purse was worth "at least $100," and suggested that it be sold at a consignment store. Mari Gold said she had tried that before but after the consignment store took it's cut, the shop didn't make much more than it would have in the first place. "Just not worth the effort," she'd say.

This woman worked at an annual church flea market, so she made it a point to know what things were worth. She showed Mari Gold glassware that was "Waterford," pointing to the teeny tiny mark, using a magnifier, and suggested that it should be priced higher than other glassware.

Another customer advised that a gold leaf pin displayed in the glass case, marked only $1.00, was "real gold," and she was certain that it came from a place at the Natick Mall where years ago they dipped real leaves in real gold. Other experts often examined jewelry or glassware and remarked that the shop should be asking more money.

A gentleman, who purchased books on a regular basis, often commented that the shop should be asking more money for them. He usually gave a donation in addition to the fifty cents being asked for hardcovers. At the time, paperbacks sold for 25 cents and hardcovers, even ones with new jackets, showing upwards of a $25 price, sold for 50 cents. The hardcovers were eventually marked up to $1.00.

When Butter Kupp, who had been an art teacher, first began volunteering at the shop, she was stunned the first time she saw a very nice book on art being sold for $1.00. She expressed the opinion that the book had probably originally cost at least $50, and suggested that the better books be priced higher.

The Crafty Ladies

Naturally, people who are into crafting, creative repurposing and the like, frequent places like thrift shops. This pastime seems to have reached an epidemic level.

One such customer told the volunteers that she worked at a nursing home. She claimed that she decorated tables and made crafts with the elderly residents. She bought up holiday items like tablecloths, napkins and decorations, material, sewing notions, and the like, but also was on the lookout for various collectibles.

Mari Gold suspected that this woman did more than just entertain people at a nursing home, not that she considered what the woman did with her purchases any of her business. But, the volume of stuff she bought lent suspicion that she was up to more than decorating tables. Just for the heck of it, Mari Gold put one of the new volunteers up to inquiring if she had a shop or sold things on line. She stuck to her guns, maintaining that she just used all the stuff herself.

Hosta and others often noted, "It was all donated anyway," so what did it matter. But some volunteers were annoyed at the thought of someone making money off of what they bought at the shop.

Thrift Shop customers often frequented another store in town which dealt with donations of used items. Some of the ladies considered their operation as competition, even relishing comments by customers that the other store wasn't nearly as neat and orderly. Mari Gold didn't see it that way. She would point out that the other store received donations by the truckload, so it was more difficult to keep everything neat and organized. Besides, the other store was in business to help people who were down and out in five or six nearby towns. They had paid help, but also lots of volunteers. They were a much bigger operation and accepted and sold a lot of furniture — something the Thrift Shop did not have space for. Mari Gold just couldn't see why the ladies would view them as "competition." Again, why did it matter. They were performing a needed service to the community.

Another buyer of miscellaneous "junk" admitted to having a corner at a consignment store, especially after Mari Gold mentioned having seen it. She often brought donations, some having been previously purchased from the shop. She sought out funky things. She had the habit of poking her head into the back room, ducking under the "Employees Only" sign to sneak a peek. "What's new? Any good jewelry?" This annoyed Scarlet no end. At some point she was asked to refrain from this practice. Other customers did the same, especially ones who were using the dressing room.

Some customers bought old sewing patterns, Simplicity, McCalls, Butterick, etc., catalogs or magazines about knitting or crocheting — things Hosta was convinced nobody would possibly want. It was amazing how the smallest scraps of material, buttons, various trim pieces, and all kinds of notions would sell, unless, of course, Hosta got her hands on them beforehand.

A man came to the shop one Christmas asking if there were any snow globes for sale. Mari Gold showed him one or two nice ones. Then he asked if there were any others, and was told there were a few that were being thrown away because the insides had become cloudy or dirty. "I'll take them," he replied, explaining that he broke the glass on the globes and rescued the little people or buildings inside to add to his Christmas village. Mari Gold thought that was a great idea — always in favor of finding a use for things that other folks thought useless.

Christmas at the Thrift Shop

Christmas donations were always plentiful and came into the shop year round. Scarlett placed holiday decorations (Valentine's, St. Patricks's, Easter, 4ᵗʰ of July, Halloween, Thanksgiving, etc.) into boxes marked with the particular holiday. When the box was full, she'd have one of her helpers move it onto a storage shelf. Christmas donations had their very own large storage closet, and by fall, the closet would be packed to the ceiling, box on top of box.

When Mari Gold first started decorating the windows, she found it difficult to unstack and weed through all the boxes to find what she was looking for. She liked to specialize her Christmas theme, choosing a different one each year.

In an effort to make this job more efficient time-wise, one summer she spent several very hot afternoons when the shop was closed organizing the boxes so like things would be together — Santas, snowmen, angels, sleighs, candles, lights, ceramic items, wrapping paper and ribbon, etc. This effort helped to some degree, but with Christmas donations coming in year round, it made the task of keeping things organized nearly impossible.

Shortly after Dora Bell took over as chairman, she found a large plastic choo choo train at a yard sale. She thought it would be great to use in the Christmas window. It came with a very long interlocking track, most likely meant to be set up in someone's yard. Mari Gold used as much of the track as she could, running it up the wall and around the floor of window. She chose various stuffed animals to ride the train as Santa's helpers. A sign was made, identifying it as the North Pole Express.

The train received lots of attention from customers, many of whom inquired if it was for sale. Dora was insistent that it be kept as a signature piece, similar to what department stores like Macy's did for the holidays. For four years, Mari Gold used the train in the window, changing up the placement to create a fresh look. Every year, customers would ask, "How much is the train?"

"It's not for sale," they were told. And so it went, until its last Christmas. Mari Gold wanted to do something different, and the train and track were taking up valuable real estate in the Christmas closet. A lady who worked at the local hospital told Mari Gold the train would be perfect for her two-year-old grandson. So, the train was sold much to Dora's dismay.

Another year, Mari Gold got a bright idea to create a scene using angels since quite a few had congregated in the Christmas storage area. There were also numerous thin white nylon sheer curtains on hand, so she made a backdrop using the filmy white curtains. Little white lights were strung around the perimeter of the window, with angels and angel-related items placed here and there. White and silver stars and snowflakes were dropped from the ceiling using thin thread. It turned out rather heavenly.

Usually Christmas decorations were kept in their closet until after Thanksgiving. Volunteers and customers alike thought putting decorations out before that simply was unChristian. Mari Gold was in complete agreement for her first couple of years. But Christmas donations were so numerous that it just seemed sensible to start selling them as early as possible, like right after Halloween. Some of the volunteers and some of the customers protested, but those in favor just chanted, "all the other stores are doing it."

A Christmas-in-July window was introduced the year that the hospital celebrated its 125th anniversary. As part of the year-long celebration, the hospital arranged with the local theater to show "The Christmas Story" in July. People were handed free popcorn with a fortune cookie on top, and the famous leg lamp was part of the raffle.

The Thrift Shop was just across the street from the theater so it seemed a good idea to decorate the window as part of the celebration. While the show was a success, the sales at the shop met with only mediocre response. The effort of decorating the window with a Christmas theme in July was repeated the following year, but it was even less successful — certainly not worth digging all the Christmas stuff out of boxes in the back room, which then just had to be packed away again until October or November.

Hosta occasionally suggested that a moratorium be declared on accepting Christmas donations, especially when the closet was almost full by June. A sign would be posted for the volunteers not to accept Christmas donations until further notice. The trouble was donators would bring in really good stuff which most of the volunteers didn't think should be turned down.

"We need a bigger store," Hosta would suggest. Mari Gold felt strongly that the shop should remain on Main Street where it had always been. A couple other locations were considered at times, but the spaces available never seemed to fit the shop's needs and requirements. So the ladies continued to work hard to keep the shop as organized as possible, often rearranging shelving units and racks to make the limited space work better.

This and That

Once in awhile a customer, or someone making a donation, would mention that their mother had worked in the Thrift Shop in the past. When one such donor mentioned her mother's name, Mari Gold told her she was pictured with a group of ladies in a newspaper article framed and hanging on the wall in the back room. When Mari Gold showed it to the woman, she said that four of the six women in the photo had gone to school together and had worked in the shop for many years. Two of them had been co-chairs of the shop for about 20 years. It was always nice when people shared stories like this one.

On occasion, customers have talked about their travels. One group of women was in town to visit the Russian Icon Museum. For a small town, there were some pretty amazing places to visit. Besides the Russian Museum there was an African Art museum, both started up by a local businessman who often visited Russia. Years before, he started collecting Russian Icons, which eventually took up so much space in his home that his wife suggested he put them in a museum. So he bought a local historic building and did just that.

Anyway, two of the ladies said they had just discovered that they were long lost cousins after one of them had recently visited Hungary and the Ukraine with another family member who was looking into her genealogy.

"One day I got a call from this woman who said she was my cousin. I thought it was a crank call, but she convinced me to stay on the line while she explained how she knew we were cousins. Now, we are having a great time getting to know each other." Mari Gold said she thought it was amazing how cousins just connect. All her cousins lived in different states and didn't get to see each other but once ever 10 or 20 years. When they did manage a reunion, it was like they'd been together all along.

A few years ago, a very expensive-looking Nun doll, complete with a cross around her neck and rosary beads in her hands, was donated. She stood about four feet high. Someone came up with the idea of holding a raffle, rather than just selling her outright. Rosie was President of the Guild at the time and was instructed (probably by Scarlet) to look into the legality of holding a raffle.

A case was built to display her and keep her clean. It was made of wood on three sides, and plexiglass on the front. Raffle tickets were sold for a couple of months, but there really wasn't an over-abundance of interest. Eventually, the drawing was held and Rosie's friend Petunia won the doll. After the expense of making her display case, the Nun doll brought in a whopping $28. There haven't been any raffles since.

Several years ago the shop saw an influx of wedding gowns. Since wedding gowns weren't an easy sell, a decision was made to offer them free to military brides-to-be. An article appeared in the local paper to get the word out. The dresses were described as "ranging from stark white to cream shades, with classic, pearled and beaded styles in sizes small to medium." The short write-up went on to say that "a few have cathedral-length trains, veils, or full bouffant half-slips." It was noted that one of the six dresses on hand had never been worn. There was no record, however, of how many brides-to-be took the shop up on the offer.

As mentioned earlier, there was a gym a couple of doors down from the thrift shop. On Tuesday, Wednesday and Thursday mornings the "Silver Sneakers" people met for an exercise class. Everyone wasn't necessarily a "Silver Sneakers" card holder but the owners of the gym offered the class to any senior for only $1.00 a day.

When the women who attended the class were returning to their cars, many walked by the Thrift Shop and often could be seen peaking in the windows. Some ventured in. Some bought an item or two, and several began to donate things.

One lady, who loved puzzles, often bought a couple she hadn't done before. Then she donated the ones she no longer wanted. Another woman bought tea cups for family members if their birthday month was on the cup. And still another belonged to a church where the choir held a special themed tea each year. She bought up colorful beads for a Mardi Gras tea, and the next year, a rose garland and horse pin for a Kentucky Derby theme.

Thank God for Dandy Lyon

During one of Mari Gold's last year's at the Thrift Shop, as she was getting ready to decorate the windows, and the store, for Christmas, an acquaintance of hers dropped by. Mari Gold mentioned how she was beginning to feel she needed assistance, especially with the windows and especially at Christmastime. A few days later, Dandy Lyon called and offered to help out.

"That's great," Mari Gold said, "But, you'll have to pay $5.00 to become a Guild member first." Yearly dues were $5.00 and Guild membership was required of the volunteers. Dandy Lyon was fine with that.

Dandy Lyon came by her name because she was deep rooted in the community, and was topped off with a puff of fluffy hair, although it wasn't white. No matter. Like Mari Gold, she had a varied background, having been a teacher, store owner, and real estate broker. Mari Gold's background had been stenographer/legal secretary, newspaper reporter/feature story writer, and interior decorator. Both were overflowing with ideas, energetic for their age, and willing to work for nothing.

Dandy Lyon began working with Mari Gold and Hosta on

Monday afternoons, but it wasn't long before she was dropping in with donations and staying to help out on other days. This new enthusiast made Mari Gold and Hosta's hearts jump for joy.

Having owned a clothes store for several years, she was a great help in that department. She reinvented the "designer label" rack. She suggested that when these items were placed on display in the window, or around the shop, that special tags be used to identify the designer, with the size and price noted.

She set aside designer handbags, which she looked up on line to determine their value and then suggested a good and reasonable price for them. If they were to be displayed in the window, she made a tented card to identify them, although Mari Gold thought the cards would just get knocked over and/ or misplaced.

She also had worked for a jeweler and knew how to spot the good stuff — identifying silver or gold by numbers engraved into the pieces. It was always helpful when the volunteers were educated about things that were sold in the shop. She discovered a silver stick pin with a little apple decoration which she thought might be valuable. When she looked it up, she found that it was from Tiffany's.

One day, Dandy Lyon brought in a collection of an artist's prints which were drawn for calendar use. The prints were of various beautiful flowers, but naturally had a corresponding month printed on them. Dandy Lyon had noticed a large number of picture frames sitting around. She thought it would be a good idea to match the prints up with the frames. She worked for hours cutting out just the right print for a complimentary frame. When Mari Gold suggested the project was taking an awful lot of time, given what they would be priced, Dandy Lyon quickly retorted, "We're here anyway. Might as well be doing something useful."

Mari Gold told her that she, and others, had spent time over the years, both at the shop and at home, making things more appealing to a buyer. They soon learned, however, that it really wasn't worth all the effort when things sold so cheap. It was always refreshing, though, to see an enthusiastic newcomer.

Eventually the framed prints sold, but only for $1.00 apiece. One buyer actually had family members with birthdays in June, July and November, three of the months that found their way into frames.

Dandy Lyon's enthusiasm reinvigorated Mari Gold for awhile, but it wasn't long before she found herself running out of steam and wanting to move on. With the arrival of Dandy Lyon she felt the Thrift Shop had found her replacement. Who knows, after 10 years or so, Dandy Lyon might write a book too.

About the Author

After spending her last 20 years of employment as an interior decorator, Marjorie Burke joined the ranks of retirees looking for ways to use their new found freedom. When she discovered that a little thrift shop, in business to benefit the local hospital, needed volunteers, she decided to join its ranks. Maintaining her almost life-long passion for writing, she began jotting down stories about the colorful characters, both volunteers who worked in the shop, and customers who were frequent visitors. They seemed to give her plenty of material to write about, and now she has put these stories into her book, Little Shop of Flowers. Previous to working at a wallpaper and paint store, the author worked as a local newspaper reporter, covering town meetings and writing feature stores. For eight years, she wrote the featured farm story in the Bolton (MA) Fair Book, and also had articles published in Plus Magazine, in San Luis Obispo, CA, and the Loyalhanna Review in Ligonier, PA. She published her first book, Keeping in Touch, in 2005, followed by Tales From an Orphanage in 2009.

www.ingramcontent.com/pod-product-compliance
Lightning Source LLC
Chambersburg PA
CBHW050419290526
45786CB00003B/1327